This book belongs to

....

b small

Published by b small publishing ltd.
www.bsmall.co.uk
© b small publishing ltd. 2024

1 2 3 4 5

All rights reserved.
No reproduction, copy or transmission of this publication may be made without written permission. No part of this publication may be reproduced, stored in a retrieval system or transmitted in any form or by any means, electronic, mechanical, photocopying, recording or otherwise, without the prior permission of the publisher.

Printed in China by WKT Co. Ltd. on FSC-certified paper, supporting responsible forestry.

Editorial: Sam Hutchinson
Design: Vicky Barker

ISBN 978-1-916851-16-0

British Library Cataloguing-in-Publication Data.
A catalogue record for this book is available from the British Library.

MY FIRST ENGLISH PICTURE WORD BOOK

CATHERINE BRUZZONE & VICKY BARKER

b small

Contents

🦆	Animals	4
🕐	At home	8
👞	Clothes	10
🍎	Colours	14
👧	Family	18

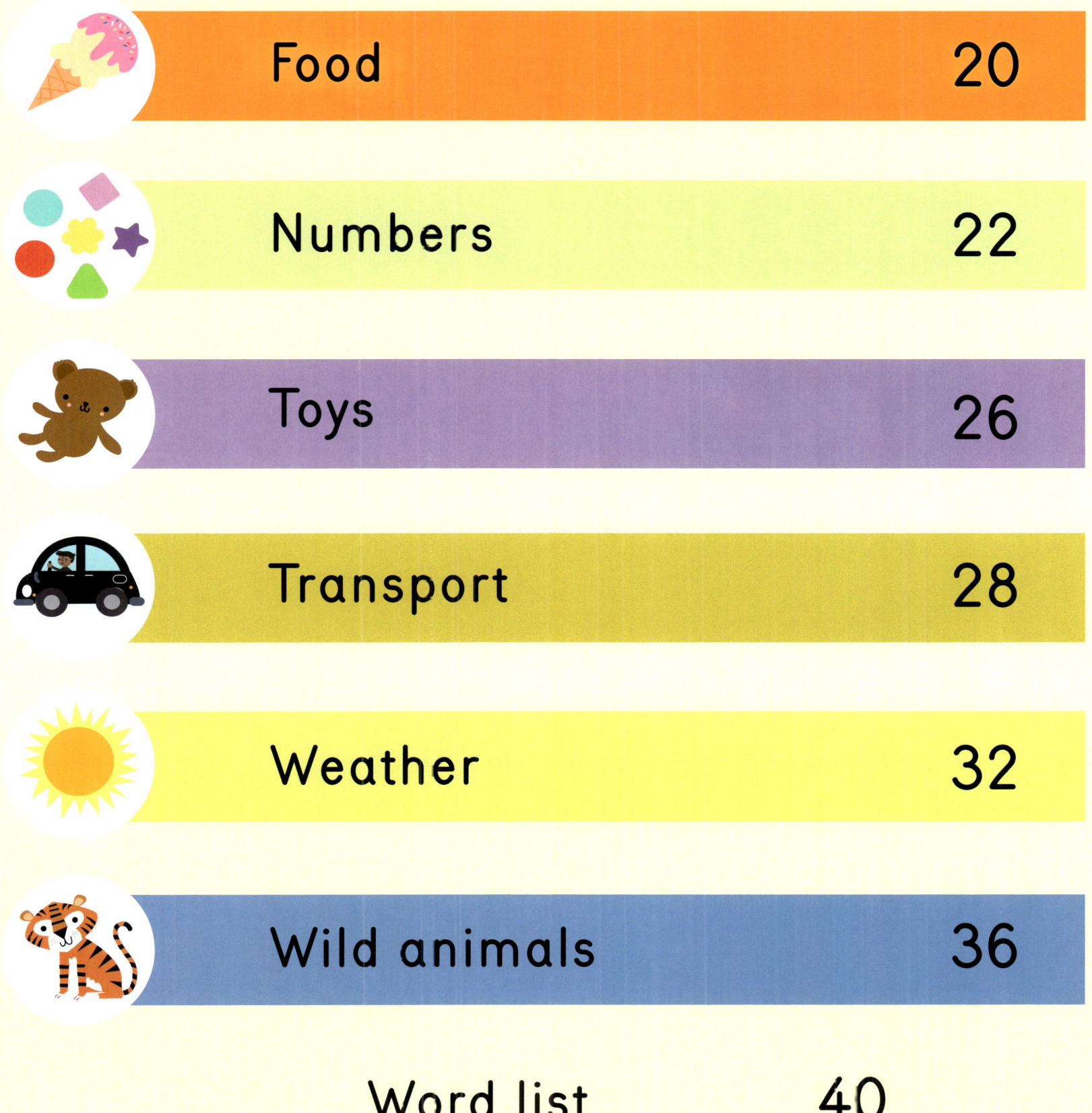

Food	20
Numbers	22
Toys	26
Transport	28
Weather	32
Wild animals	36

Word list   40

Animals

cat

mouse

horse

dog

cow

5

rabbit

fish

sheep

chicken

goat

goose

pig

At home

window

clock
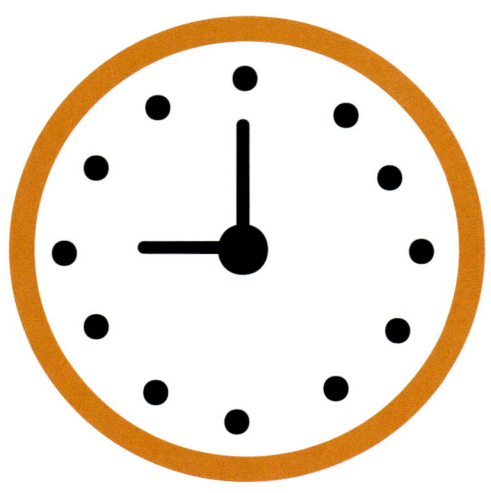

door

bed

fridge

bath

light

shower

water

Clothes

skirt

vest

jumper

T-shirt

shoes

dress

cardigan

shirt

trousers

hat

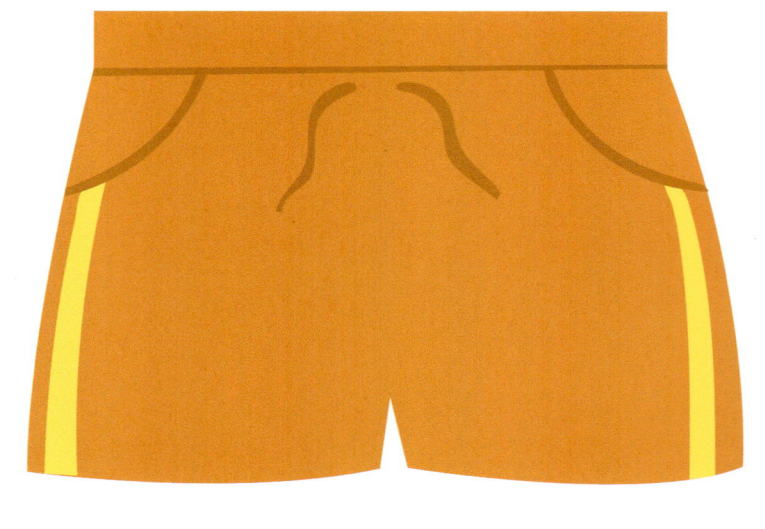

shorts

Colours

green

red

pink

black

white

yellow

purple

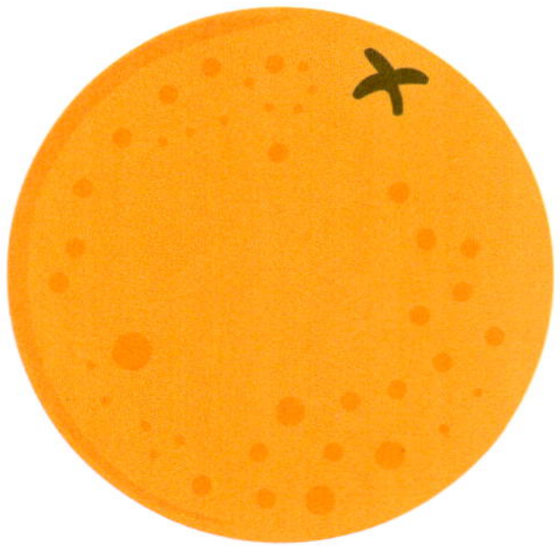

orange

Family

mother

father

brother

sister

grandmother

grandfather

aunt

uncle

Food

bread

meat

fruit

vegetables

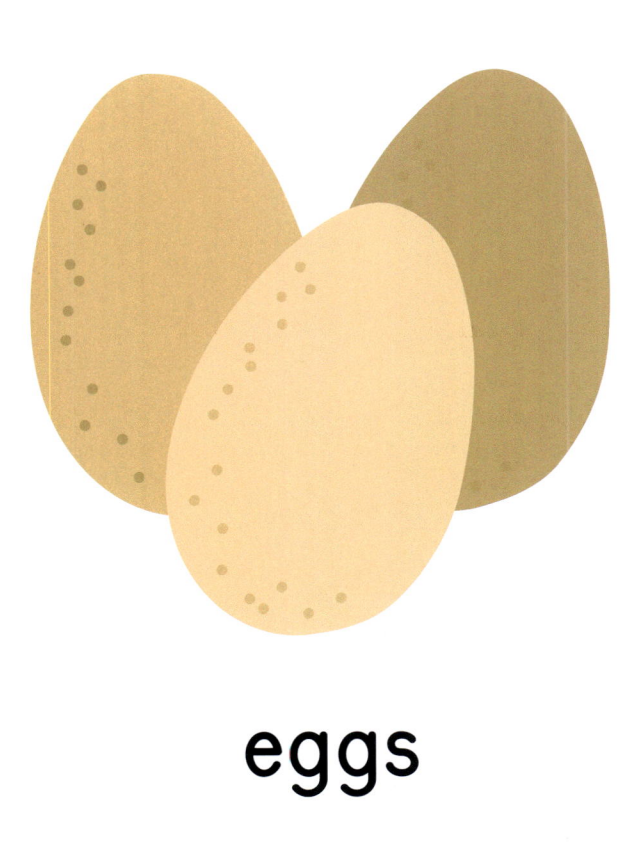

eggs

ice-cream

milk

cheese

Numbers

1 one

2 two

3 three

4 four

5 five

6 six

7 seven

8 eight

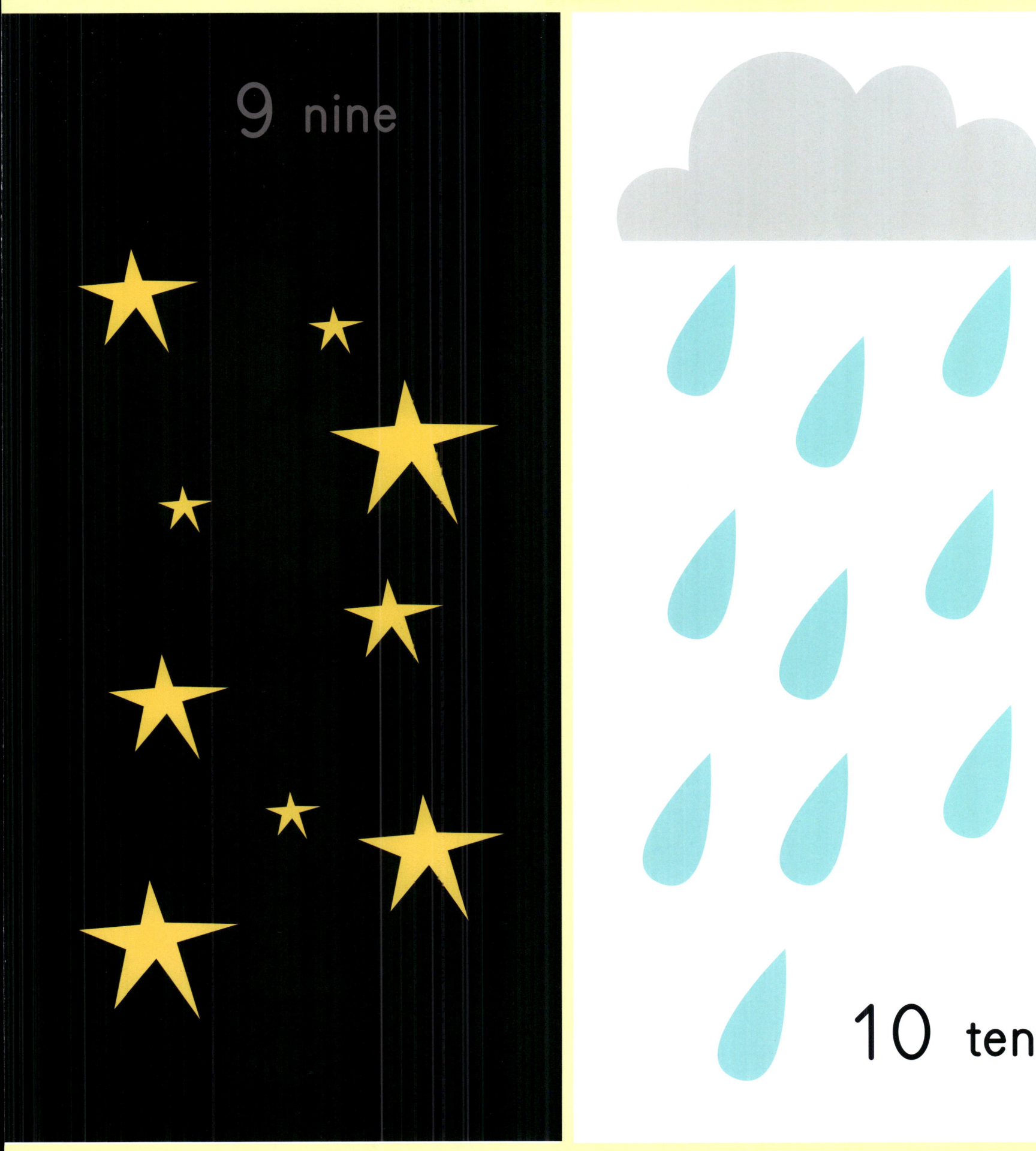

Toys

ball

teddy bear

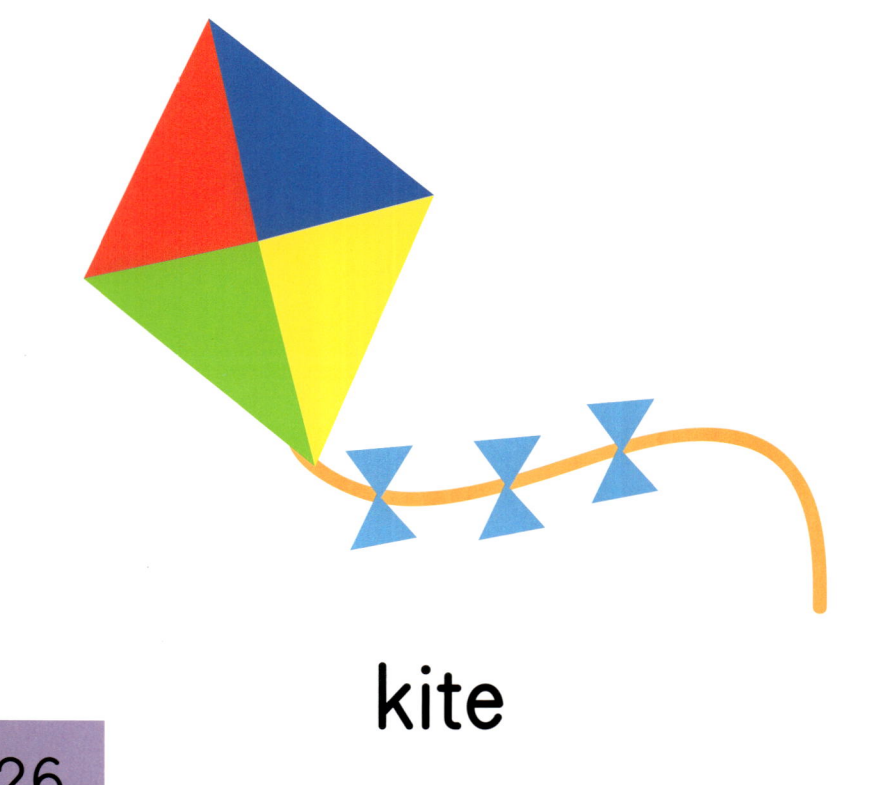
kite

blocks

doll

jigsaw

coloured pencils

book

Transport

bicycle

motorbike

bus

car

police car

aeroplane

ambulance

train

tractor

fire engine

lorry

digger

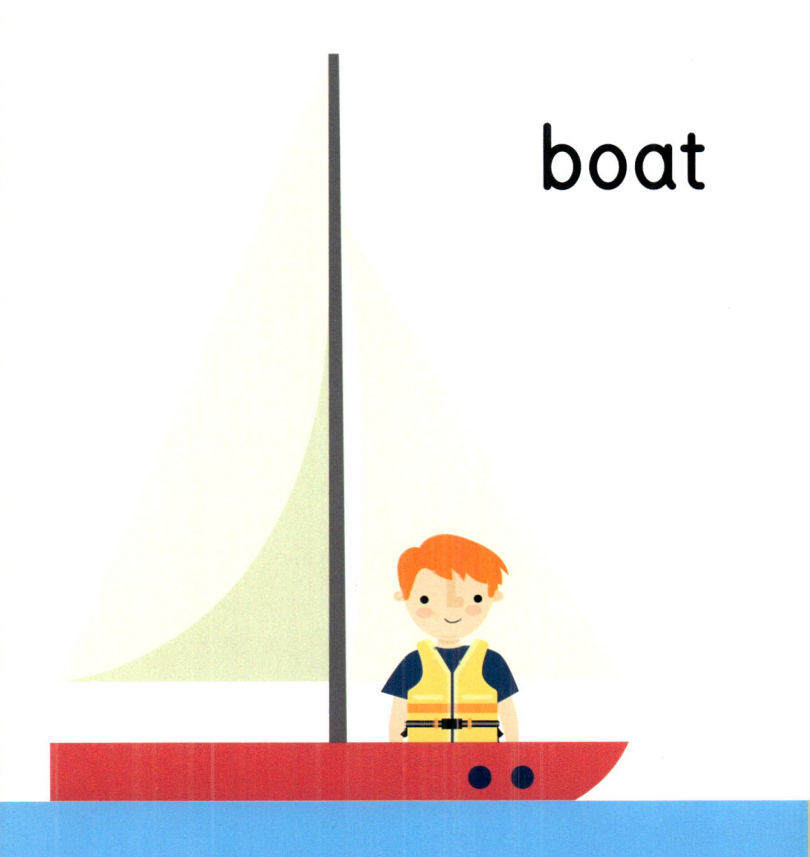

boat

Weather

sun

rain

snow

cloud

wind

storm

thunder

fog

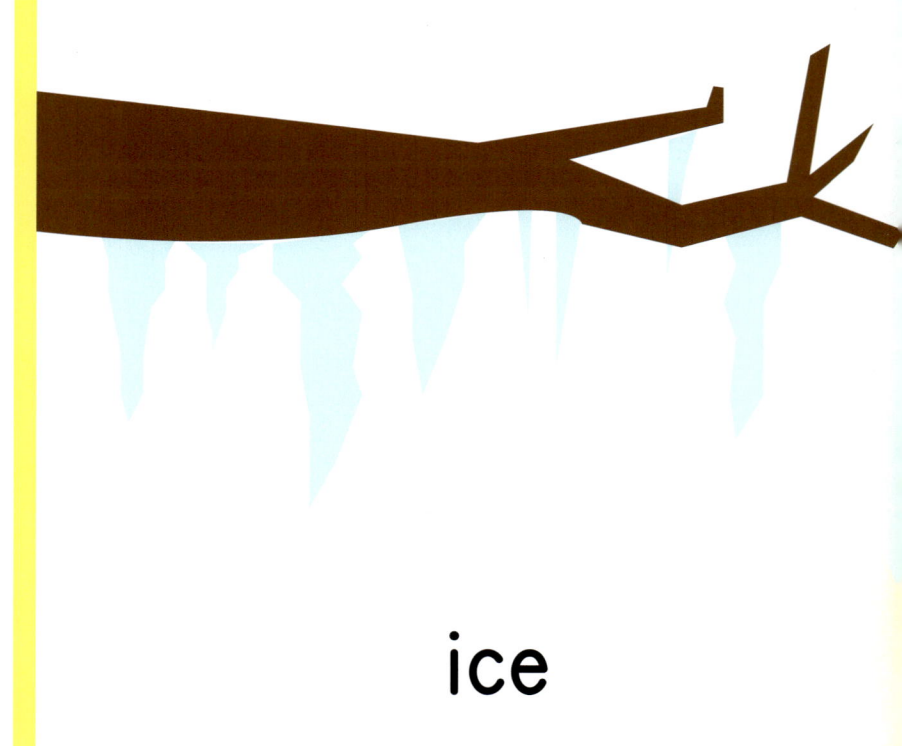

ice

lightning

rainbow

Wild animals

snake

giraffe

hippopotamus

tiger

elephant

brown bear

penguin

zebra

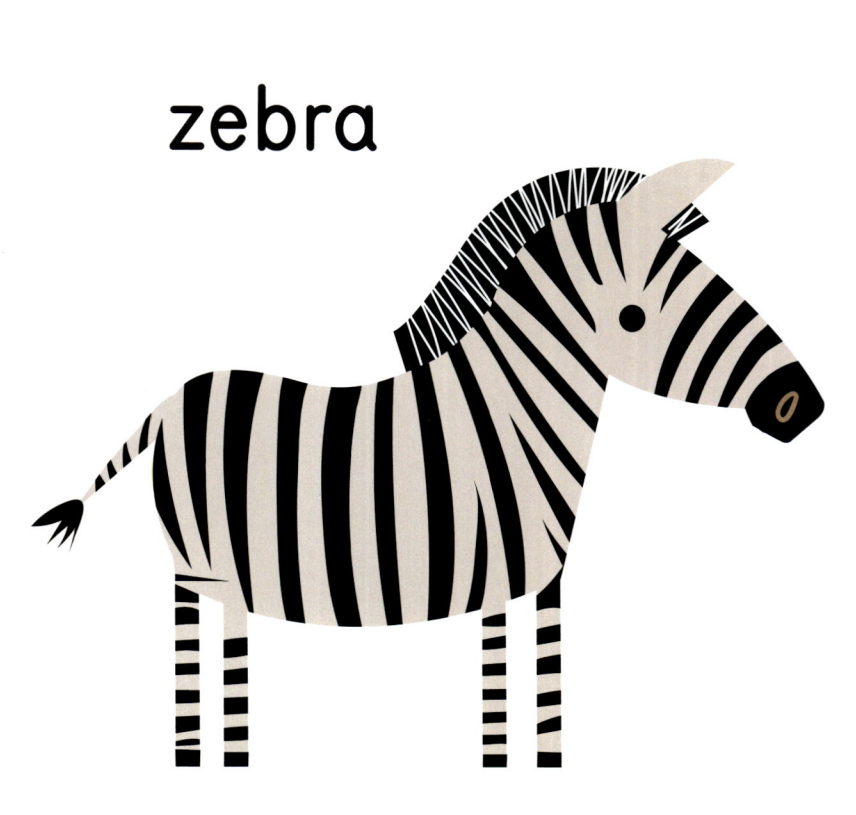

monkey

lion

crocodile

kangaroo

polar bear

panda

Word list

aeroplane	car	duck	grandmother
ambulance	cardigan	eggs	green
animals	cat	eight	grey
aunt	cheese	elephant	hat
ball	chicken	family	hippopotamus
bath	clock	father	home
bed	clothes	fire engine	horse
bicycle	cloud	fish	ice
black	coat	five	ice-cream
blocks	coloured pencils	fog	jigsaw
blue	colours	food	jumper
boat	cow	four	kangaroo
book	crocodile	fridge	kite
bread	digger	fruit	light
brother	dog	giraffe	lightning
brown	doll	goat	lion
brown bear	door	goose	lorry
bus	dress	grandfather	meat

milk	rain	ten	wind
monkey	rainbow	three	window
mother	red	thunder	yellow
motorbike	seven	tiger	zebra
mouse	sheep	toys	
nine	shirt	tractor	
numbers	shoes	train	
one	shorts	transport	
orange	shower	trousers	
panda	sister	T-shirt	
penguin	six	two	
pig	skirt	uncle	
pink	snake	vegetables	
polar bear	snow	vest	
police car	socks	water	
purple	storm	weather	
pyjamas	sun	white	
rabbit	teddy bear	wild animals